On Passover

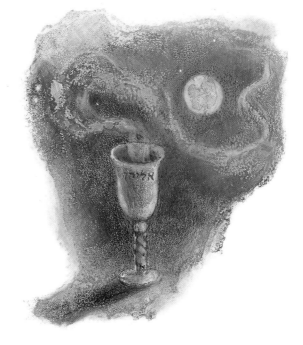

On Passover

BY

CATHY GOLDBERG FISHMAN

ILLUSTRATED BY

MELANIE W. HALL

ALADDIN PAPERBACKS

First Aladdin Paperbacks edition February 2000

Text copyright © 1997 by Cathy Goldberg Fishman
Illustrations copyright © 1997 by Melanie W. Hall

Aladdin Paperbacks
An imprint of Simon & Schuster Children's Publishing Division
1230 Avenue of the Americas
New York, NY 10020

Also available in an Atheneum Books for Young Readers hardcover edition.
The text for this book was set in Novarese.
The illustrations were rendered in collagraph and mixed media.
Printed in Hong Kong
2 4 6 8 10 9 7 5 3 1

The Library of Congress has cataloged the hardcover edition as follows:
Fishman, Cathy Goldberg.
On Passover / by Cathy Goldberg Fishman ; illustrated by Melanie W. Hall. — 1st ed.
p.   cm.
Summary: As her family prepares for Passover, a little girl learns about the many traditions
which are part of the celebration of this holiday.
ISBN: 0-689-80528-4 (hc.)
1. Passover—Juvenile literature. [1. Passover.] I. Hall, Melanie W. II. Title.
BM695.P3F57   1997
296.4'37—dc20
91-43110
ISBN 0-689-83264-8 (Aladdin pbk.)

To the memory of my grandmother,
Hannabelle Hirsch Goldberg
—C. G. F.

For my sisters Carolyn and Pamela
—M. W. H.

I hear my father singing in a deep, rumbly voice. "Dy-dy-enu, *dy-dy-enu*," he sings in Hebrew. "It would be enough." His song is loud and happy. I know it is time to get ready for Passover.

I help my mother carry boxes out of the closet. Every year I help and every year I ask, "What's in this box?"

"Use your eyes and find out," my mother always answers.

So I do. Very carefully, I cut the string, lift the lid and I can see Passover! I see the *Seder plate*, decorated with pictures of parsley, bitter herbs, an egg, and a roasted bone—for springtime, sorrow, life, and ancient traditions. I see the dishes and pots and pans that we use only on Passover. In another box I find a candle, a feather, and a spoon.

This year I ask another question: "What is Passover?"

"Passover is a Jewish holiday," Mother says. "For one whole week during the Hebrew month of Nisan we will eat special Passover food on special Passover dishes. We'll clean the house very carefully and remove all of the *leavened bread* that we eat every day."

That night we light the candle and carry it around the darkened house. The flame sends shadow people dancing on the walls as the feather sweeps forgotten bits of leavened bread into the spoon. I see the candle glowing as we welcome Passover.

If Passover had only things to see, I think, dyenu—it would be enough. But Passover has things to smell, too.

"What's in the pot?" I always ask my grandmother as she cooks.

"Use your nose and find out," she always smiles and answers.

So I do. I stand in the middle of the steamy kitchen and sniff and sniff until I can smell Passover! I smell chicken soup and *gefilte fish*. I smell apples, nuts, and cinnamon. I smell spring as the earth welcomes new life.

This year I ask another question: "Why do you mix the apples and nuts together?"

"The mixture of apples and nuts is called *charoses*," Grandmother says. "It reminds us of the mortar we used to build the great cities when we were slaves in Egypt."

If Passover had only things to see and things to smell, I think, dyenu—it would be enough. But Passover has things to taste.

Every year my sisters help Grandmother in the kitchen. "What's that?" I always ask them, pointing to the food.

"Use your tongue and find out," they always tease.

So I do. The crunchy *matzah* crumbles dryly on my tongue and I can taste Passover! I taste tears of sorrow in the salt water. I taste new life in the parsley. I taste the bitterness of slavery in the horseradish.

This year I ask them: "Why do we eat this food on Passover?"

"When we escaped from Egypt," they answer, "we were in such a hurry that we didn't have time to let our bread rise or cook properly. We called it matzah, the bread of freedom. Every year we eat the matzah and the bitter herbs and the parsley to help us remember what happened to us a long time ago."

If Passover only had things to see and things to smell and things to taste, I think, dyenu—it would be enough. But Passover has things to hear.

"What's in that book?" I always ask, giggling, because I really know.

"Use your ears and find out," my brother always says.

So I do. I open the *Haggadah*, the Passover service book, and I can hear Passover! I hear my father say the blessing over the matzah. He breaks off half and goes to hide it.

"The child who finds this *afikomen*," he says, "will get a present." But I know that he will have presents for everyone.

"*Mah nish-ta-nah ha-ly-lah ha-zeh.*" I hear my brother sing his questions. And I hear the plagues God inflicted upon the Egyptians chanted. I dip my finger in the Passover wine and let ten drops fall, one by one, as each plague is named. I hear the songs and blessings of the Haggadah sung around the table.

This year I ask my brother: "What are you singing?"

"I am singing the 'Four Questions,'" he answers. "They ask why this night is different from all other nights."

"I know," I say. "I know why. Because we eat matzah, not leavened bread. And we eat bitter herbs and remember the story of Passover."

"Yes," says my father. "It's very important that we celebrate Passover every year. Every year we talk about what happened when we were slaves so that we won't forget what it feels like to be mistreated. We talk about it so we'll remember not to mistreat others and to pray for all of the people in the world who don't have freedom."

If Passover had only things to see and things to smell and things to taste and things to hear, I think, dyenu—it would be enough. But Passover has things to feel.

My father stands at the head of the table. Every year he plays my game. With his hands over my eyes, he always asks, "What's this? Use your fingers and find out."

So I do. I stretch out my arms and let my fingers stroke the silken matzah cover. I can feel Passover! I feel the softness of the cushions reminding us that we were once slaves, but now we are free.

I feel the smooth coolness of Elijah the Prophet's special silver cup. I wonder if he will come this year and drink the wine set aside for him.

"What else is Passover?" I ask.

"Passover is a time for you to ask questions, listen to the answers, and for all of you to find the afikomen," says Father with a smile.

So we do. We look and look throughout the house
and I find the afikomen and we all get our Passover
presents.

My father says that Passover is a time to ask questions. So I do. And I listen to the answers. But this year I think that Passover is most of all a wonderful feeling in my heart, dyenu.

And next year it will be the same.

Glossary

Afikomen (ah fee KO mun): one of three pieces of matzah on the Seder table. The middle piece is broken in half and hidden. This hidden piece of matzah is called the afikomen. In Jewish tradition, the Passover meal cannot be concluded until everyone has shared in the eating of the afikomen.

Charoses (kha RO sis) or (ha RO sis): usually a mixture of nuts, apples, wine, and spices that symbolizes the mortar used by the Israelite slaves.

Dyenu (da YEA nu): part of a prayer sung in the Haggadah. It means "it would be enough."

Gefilte fish (ga FILL ta FISH): a mixture of pike and whitefish, chopped and combined with onions, matzah meal, eggs, and spices, shaped into patties and cooked.

Haggadah (ha GAH da): a special book that tells the story of Passover through prayers and songs.

Leavened bread (LEV end BRED): bread or other grain products that have been made with yeast or that have come in contact with water for more than eighteen minutes.

Mah nish-ta-nah ha-ly-lah ha-zeh (MAH nish ta nah ha LIE la ha zeh): the transliteration in Hebrew of part of the first question, "Why is this night different from all other nights?"

Matzah (MA tza): a cracker-like bread made without yeast and cooked very quickly.

Nisan (NEE san): the first month of the ancient Hebrew calendar. It corresponds to March/April.

Seder (SAY dur): a term used for the Passover meal. It means order and refers to the prayers and songs sung before and after the meal.

Seder plate (SAY dur PLAYT): a specially decorated plate holding the symbolic foods used at the Seder table.